The Essential Keto Cookbook

Discover How To Feel Great With Healthy And Appetizing Recipes

Valerie Naviolet

© Copyright 2021 by Valerie Naviolet- All rights reserved.

The following Book is reproduced below to provide information that is as accurate and reliable as possible. Regardless, purchasing this Book can be seen as consent to the fact that both the publisher and the author of this book are in no way experts on the topics discussed within and that any recommendations or suggestions that are made herein are for entertainment purposes only. Professionals should be consulted as needed before undertaking any of the actions endorsed herein.

This declaration is deemed fair and valid by both the American Bar Association and the Committee of Publishers Association and is legally binding throughout the United States.

Furthermore, the transmission, duplication, or reproduction of any of the following work including specific information will be considered an illegal act irrespective of if it is done electronically or in print. This extends to creating a secondary or tertiary copy of the work or a recorded copy and is only allowed with the express written consent from the Publisher. All additional rights reserved.

The information in the following pages is broadly considered a truthful universal. As befitting its nature, it is presented without assurance regarding its prolonged validity or interim quality. Trademarks that are mentioned are done without written consent and can in no way be considered an endorsement from the trademark holder. and accurate account of facts and as such, any inattention, use, or misuse of the information in question by the reader will render any resulting actions solely under their purview. There are no scenarios in which the publisher or the original author of this work can be in any fashion deemed liable for any hardship or damages that may befall them after undertaking the information described herein.

Additionally, the information in the following pages is intended only for informational purposes and should thus be thought of as

Contents

Introduction 8
Chapter 1 : Breakfast Recipes 10
    Skillet Based Kale And Avocado 10
    Fat Burner Espresso 12
    Blue Cheese Omelet 14
    Hearty Chia Bowls 16
    Classical Eggs And Canadian Bacon 18
    Pecan And Goat Cheese 20
Chapter 2 : Appetizer and Snacks Recipes 22
    Spicy Pimento Cheese Dip 22
    Bacon Smoky Doodles 24
    Tantalizing Butter Beans 26
    Walnuts And Asparagus Delight 28
    Spicy Chili Crackers 30
Chapter 3 : Poultry Recipes 32
    Balsamic Chicken 32
    Low- Carb Butternut Chicken 35
    The Original Greek Chicken Breast 37
    Chicken Ham And Turnip Pasta 39
    The Perfect Winter Turkey Goulash 41
Chapter 4 : Beef Recipes 43
    Mushroom And Olive "Mediterranean" Steak 43
    Satisfying Low-Carb Beef Liver Salad 45
    Perfect Aromatic Beef Roast 47

Beef Packed Zucchini Boats..49

Spicy Chipotle Steak.. 51

Chapter 5 : Fish and Seafood Recipes........................53

Grilled Lime Shrimp 53

Mouthwatering Calamari 55

Salmon And Zesty Cream Sauce 57

Crisped Up Coconut Shrimp 59

Spiced Up Tuna Avocado Balls... 61

Chapter 6 : Soups and Stews Recipes 63

Clean Chicken And Mushroom Stew 63

Hearty Keto Chicken And Egg Soup 65

Ingenious Eggplant Soup 67

Amazing Roasted Carrot Soup 69

The Brussels's Fever..71

Chapter 7 : Vegan and Vegetarian Recipes 73

Hearty Green Bean Roast... 73

Almond And Blistered Beans 75

Chipotle Kale Chips.. 77

Classic Guacamole 79

Astonishingly Simple Lettuce Salad 81

Chapter 8 : Desserts Recipes 83

The Easy "No-Bake" Fudge 83

Elegant Poppyseed Muffins.. 85

Swirly Cinnamon Muffins 87

Mesmerizing Garlic Bagels 89

Ravaging Blueberry Muffin 91

No-Bake Cheesecake 93

Stylish Chocolate Parfait 95

Supreme Matcha Bomb 97

Hearty Almond Bread 99

Chapter 9 : Refreshing Drinks And Smoothies 102

The Summer Hearty Shake 102

Sweet Protein And Cherry Shake.................................... 104

Iron And Protein Shake... 106

Flax And Almond Butter Smoothie 108

Leeks And Broccoli Cucumber Glass 110

Zucchini Apple Smoothie 112

Flax And Kiwi Spinach Smoothie 114

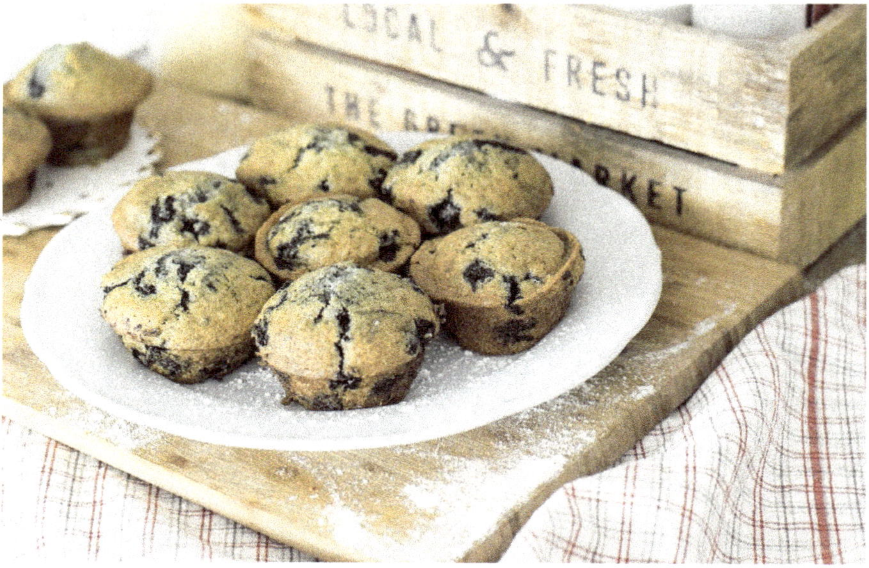
LOCAL & FRESH

i cooking *Conversion* CHARTS

Weights

Weights can be converted with the following table. Note that the ounces referred to in this table are not the same as fluid.

Quantity	Metric
1 ounce	28 g
4 ounces or 1/4 pound	113 g
1/3 pound	150 g
8 ounces or 1/2 pound	230 g
2/3 pound	300 g
12 ounces or 3/4 pound	340 g
1 pound or 16 ounces	450 g
3/4 cup or 6 fluid ounces	900 g

Oven Temperatures

Farenheit	Centigrade	Description
225 F	105 C	Very Cool
250 F	120 C	Very Cool
275 F	130 C	Cool
300 F	150 C	Cool
325 F	165 C	Very Moderate
350 F	180 C	Moderate
375 F	190 C	Moderate
400 F	200 C	Moderately Hot
425 F	220 C	Hot
450 F	230 C	Hot
475 F	245 C	Very Hot

Liquids

Liquids can be converted to liters or milliliters with the following table. Small volumes (less than about 1 fluid ounce or 2 tablespoons) of ingredients such as salt, herbs, spices, baking powder, etc. should also be converted with this table. Do not use this table to convert other non-liquid ingredients.

Quantity	Metric
1 teaspoon	5 mL
1 tablespoon or 1/2 fluid once	15 mL
1 fluid once or 1/8 cup	30 mL
1/4 cup or 2 fluid ounces	60 mL
1/3 cup	80 mL
1/2 cup or 4 fluid ounces	120 mL
2/3 cup	160 mL
3/4 cup or 6 fluid ounces	180 mL
1 cup or 8 fluid ounces or half a pint	240 mL
1 1/2 cups or 12 fluid ounces	350 mL
2 cups or 1 pint or 16 fluid ounces	475 mL
3 cups or 1 1/2 pints	700 mL
4 cups or 2 pints or 1 quart	950 mL
4 quarts or 1 gallon	3.8 L

Note: In cases where higher precision is not justified, it may be convenient to round these conversions off as follows:

1 cup = 250 mL
1 pint = 500 mL
1 quart = 1 L
1 gallon = 4 L

Introduction

This simple and practical Keto cookbook is ideal for anyone considering a Ketogenic Diet, or who simply wants to get closer to this new way of eating.

Without necessarily following a strict Keto diet, you can still benefit from the positive effects of this diet, here are just a few:

1. Inflammation issues - Ask anyone with pain issues and they will probably give you a list of food triggers that make the pain worse. This generally includes things like sugars, wheat and other grains, and starches in general.

Well, the good news is that keto nutrition removes all of these things from the menu, thus helping those with inflammation issues.

What is also noteworthy, is that many foods help with inflammation - many vegetables such as beets, nuts, tomatoes, broccoli, and many others - which are all exactly what you should be eating on a keto diet. Put like that, a keto diet for those with inflammation makes sense, doesn't it?

2. If you're an endomorph (or big-boned) and other body types that tend to store fat very easily. Let's face it, some people seem to convert everything they eat directly into fat. The good news is that a keto diet helps balance out a large body.

3. Bacon lovers - and others who love high-fat food. Since the keto diet requires you to eat things that are high in fat - the GOOD kinds of fat - then if this is something you already love and crave; you've already won half the battle.

It's always easier to use recipes that allow you to eat the foods you love the most.

4. People who have gained weight quickly - and now need to lose it

quickly. Do you still have that baby fat even though the baby is now crawling?

Did you have a long illness that made you gain weight while you were recovering? Keto can be used to get you back to your normal weight very quickly.

5. Anyone suffering from acid reflux. If you are living on a constant diet of antacids, this may be just the thing for you.

Again, the foods you eat are the ones most conducive to helping you feel better when you have constant heartburn.

If you're on that list, then it's likely that keto recipes can help reduce these situations.

The only cautions? If you are diabetic, have an eating disorder, or have had your gallbladder removed, these recipes then are not recommended.

Otherwise ....Good Appetite !!!

Chapter 1 : Breakfast Recipes

Skillet Based Kale And Avocado

Serving: 2

Prep Time: 5 minutes

Cook Time: 10 minutes

Ingredients

- 2 tablespoons olive oil, divided
- 2 cups mushrooms, sliced
- 5 ounces fresh kale, stemmed and sliced into ribbons
- 1 avocado, sliced

- 4 large eggs
- Salt and pepper as needed

How To

1. Take a large skillet and place it over medium heat

2. Add a tablespoon of olive oil

3. Add mushrooms to the pan and Saute for 3 minutes

4. Take a medium bowl and massage kale with the remaining 1 tablespoon olive oil (for about 1-2 minutes)

5. Add kale to skillet and place them on top of mushrooms

6. Place slices of avocado on top of kale

7. Create 4 wells for eggs and crack each egg onto each hold

8. Season eggs with salt and pepper

9. Cover skillet and cook for 5 minutes

10. Serve hot!

Nutrition (Per Serving)

- Calories: 461
- Fat: 34g
- Carbohydrates: 6g
- Protein: 18g

Fat Burner Espresso

Serving: 2

Prep Time: 10 minutes

Ingredients:

- 1 scoop Isopure Zero Carb protein powder
- 1 espresso shot
- ¼ cup Greek yogurt, full fat
- Liquid stevia, to sweeten
- Pinch of cinnamon
- 5 ice cubes

Directions:

1. Add listed ingredients to a blender
2. Blend until you have a smooth and creamy texture
3. Serve chilled and enjoy!

Nutritional Contents:

- Calories: 270
- Fat: 16g
- Carbohydrates: 2g
- Protein: 30g

Blue Cheese Omelet

Serving: 2

Prep Time: 10 minutes

Cook Time: 15 minutes

Ingredients

- 4 eggs
- Salt, to taste
- 1 tbsp sesame oil
- ½ cup blue cheese, crumbled
- 1 tomato, thinly sliced

How To

1. In a mixing bowl, beat the eggs and season with salt.

2. Set a saute pan over medium heat and warm the oil. Add in the eggs and cook as you swirl the eggs around the pan using a spatula.

3. Cook eggs until partially set.

4. Top with cheese; fold the omelet in half to enclose filling.

5. Decorate with tomato and serve while warm.

Nutrition (Per Serving)

- Calories: 307
- Fat: 25g
- Carbohydrates: 2.5g
- Protein: 18g

Hearty Chia Bowls

Serving: 2

Prep Time: 10 minutes

Cook Time: Nil

Ingredients

- 1/4 cup walnuts, chopped
- 1 and 1/2 cups almond milk
- 2 tablespoons chia seeds
- 1 tablespoon stevia
- 1 teaspoon vanilla extract

How To

1. In a bowl, combine the almond milk with the chia seeds and the rest of the ingredients, toss, leave the mix aside for 10 minutes and serve for breakfast

Nutrition (Per Serving)

- Calories: 300
- Fat: 8g
- Carbohydrates: 5g
- Protein: 4g

Classical Eggs And Canadian Bacon

Serving: 2

Prep Time: 10 minutes

Cook Time: 15 minutes

Ingredients

- 2 1-ounce slices of Canadian bacon
- 4 eggs
- 1/4 teaspoon ground black pepper
- Salt, to season
- 8 cherry tomatoes, halved

How To

1. Heat a nonstick aluminum pan over a medium-high flame. Once hot, fry the bacon until crispy; reserve, living the rendered fat in the pan.

2. Turn the heat to medium-low.

3. Crack the eggs into the bacon grease. Cover the pan with a lid and fry the eggs until they are cooked through.

4. Salt and pepper to taste. Serve with the reserved bacon and cherry tomatoes on the side. Enjoy!

Nutrition (Per Serving)

- Calories: 326
- Fat: 5g
- Carbohydrates: 46g
- Protein: 0.7g

Pecan And Goat Cheese

Serving: 4

Prep Time: 10 minutes

Cook Time: 10 minutes

Ingredients

- 1 lb log goat cheese
- 1/3 cup pecans, chopped
- 3 tablespoons bacon syrup
- 2 teaspoons fresh basil, chopped
- 1 teaspoon fresh chives, chopped

How To

1. In a small saucepan, add the chopped basil, bacon, and chives. Cook for 1-2 minutes and set aside.

2. Finely chop the pecans and transfer them to a large plate. Then roll the goat cheese in the chopped pecans.

3. Drizzle with the bacon mixture and serve. Enjoy

Nutrition (Per Serving)

- Calories: 296
- Fat: 8g
- Carbohydrates: 0.6g
- Protein: 14g

Chapter 2 : Appetizer and Snacks Recipes

Spicy Pimento Cheese Dip

Serving: 10

Prep Time: 5 minutes

Cook Time: 5 minutes

Ingredients

- 1 brick cream cheese
- 10 cherry peppers, chopped
- 1 and ½ cups cheddar cheese, shredded
- 1 tablespoon garlic, minced

- Black pepper to taste

How To

1. Heat garlic in a pan over medium heat

2. Drop cream cheese and let it soft, stir consistently

3. Mix in cheddar, add chopped peppers

4. Stir and enjoy with your desired dippers!

Nutrition (Per Serving)

- Calories: 259
- Fat: 24g
- Carbohydrates: 4g
- Protein: 16g

Bacon Smoky Doodles

Serving: 4

Prep Time: 5 minutes

Cook Time: 25 minutes

Ingredients

- 24 little Smokies (Sausages)
- 3 tablespoons BBQ sauce, check for Keto Friendliness
- Salt and pepper to taste
- 6 slices bacon

How To

1. Preheat your oven to 375 degrees F

2. Cut bacon into quarter pieces

3. Put sausage on each one and roll bacon over them, use a toothpick to secure it properly

4. Bake for 25 minutes and baste with BBQ sauce

5. Bake for 10 minutes more

6. Serve and enjoy!

Nutrition (Per Serving)

- Calories: 247
- Fat: 18g
- Carbohydrates: 2g
- Protein: 14g

Tantalizing Butter Beans

Serving: 4

Prep Time: 5 minutes

Cook Time: 12 minutes

Ingredients

- 2 garlic cloves, minced
- Red pepper flakes to taste
- Salt to taste
- 2 tablespoons clarified butter
- 4 cups green beans, trimmed

How To

1. Bring a pot of salted water to boil

2. Once the water starts to boil, add beans and cook for 3 minutes

3. Take a bowl of ice water and drain beans, plunge them in the ice water

4. Once cooled, keep them on the side

5. Take a medium skillet and place it over medium heat, add ghee, and melt

6. Add red pepper, salt, garlic

7. Cook for 1 minute

8. Add beans and toss until coated well, cook for 3 minutes

9. Serve and enjoy!

Nutrition (Per Serving)

- Calories: 93
- Fat: 8g
- Carbohydrates: 4g
- Protein: 2g

Walnuts And Asparagus Delight

Serving: 4

Prep Time: 5 minutes

Cook Time: 5 minutes

Ingredients

- 1 and ½ tablespoons olive oil
- ¾ pound asparagus, trimmed
- ¼ cup walnuts, chopped
- Salt and pepper to taste

How To

1. Place a skillet over medium heat add olive oil and let it heat up

2. Add asparagus, Saute for 5 minutes until browned

3. Season with salt and pepper

4. Remove heat
5. Add walnuts and toss
6. Serve warm!

Nutrition (Per Serving)

- Calories: 124
- Fat: 12g
- Carbohydrates: 2g
- Protein: 3g

Spicy Chili Crackers

Serving: 30 crackers

Prep Time: 15 minutes

Cook Time: 60 minutes

Ingredients

- ¾ cup almond flour
- ¼ cup coconut four
- ¼ cup coconut flour
- ½ teaspoon paprika
- ½ teaspoon cumin
- 1 and ½ teaspoons chili pepper spice

- 1 teaspoon onion powder
- ½ teaspoon salt
- 1 whole egg
- ¼ cup unsalted butter

How To

1. Preheat your oven to 350 degrees F
2. Take a baking sheet and line it up with parchment paper, keep it on the side
3. Add listed ingredients to food processor and process until you have a nice and firm dough
4. Divide dough into two equal parts
5. Place one ball on a sheet of parchment paper and cover it with another paper
6. Roll it out
7. Cut into crackers and do the same with the other ball
8. Transfer dough to your prepared baking dish and bake for 8-10 minutes
9. Remove from oven and serve
10. Enjoy!

Nutrition (Per Serving)

- Calories: 49
- Fat: 4.1g
- Carbohydrates: 3g
- Protein: 1.6g

Chapter 3 : Poultry Recipes

Balsamic Chicken

Serving: 6

Prep Time: 10 minutes

Cook Time: 25 minutes

Ingredients

- 6 chicken breast halves, skinless and boneless
- 1 teaspoon garlic salt
- Ground black pepper
- 2 tablespoons olive oil
- 1 onion, thinly sliced
- 14 and ½ ounces tomatoes, diced

- ½ cup balsamic vinegar
- 1 teaspoon dried basil
- 1 teaspoon dried oregano
- 1 teaspoon dried rosemary
- ½ teaspoon dried thyme

How To

1. Season both sides of your chicken breasts thoroughly with pepper and garlic salt

2. Take a skillet and place it over medium heat

3. Add some oil and cook your seasoned chicken for 3-4 minutes per side until the breasts are nicely browned

4. Add some onion and cook for another 3-4 minutes until the onions are browned

5. Pour the diced up tomatoes and balsamic vinegar over your chicken and season with some rosemary, basil, thyme, and rosemary

6. Simmer the chicken for about 15 minutes until they are no longer pink

7. Take an instant-read thermometer and check if the internal temperature gives a reading of 165 degrees Fahrenheit

8. If yes, then you are good to go!

Nutrition (Per Serving)

- Calories: 196
- Fat: 7g
- Carbohydrates: 7g
- Protein: 23g

Low- Carb Butternut Chicken

Serving: 4

Prep Time: 15 minutes

Cook Time: 30 minutes

Ingredients

- ½ pound Nitrate free bacon
- 6 chicken thighs, boneless and skinless
- 2-3 cups butternut squash, cubed
- Extra virgin olive oil
- Fresh chopped sage
- Salt and pepper as needed

How To

1. Prepare your oven by Preheating it to 425 degrees F

2. Take a large skillet and place it over medium-high heat, add bacon and fry until crispy

3. Take a slice of bacon and place it on the side, crumbled the bacon

4. Add cubed butternut squash in the bacon grease and Saute, season with salt and pepper

5. Once the squash is tender, remove the skillet and transfer to a plate

6. Add coconut oil to the skillet and add chicken thigh, cook for 10 minutes

7. Season with salt and pepper

8. Remove skillet from the stove and transfer to oven

9. Bake for 12-15 minutes, top with crumbled bacon and sage

10. Enjoy!

Nutrition (Per Serving)

- Calories: 323
- Fat: 19g
- Carbohydrates: 8g
- Protein: 12g

The Original Greek Chicken Breast

Serving: 4

Prep Time: 10 minutes

Cook Time: 25 minutes

Ingredients

- 4 chicken breast halves, skinless and boneless
- 1 cup extra virgin olive oil
- 1 lemon, juiced
- 2 teaspoons garlic, crushed
- 1 and ½ teaspoons black pepper
- 1/3 teaspoon paprika

How To

1. Cut 3 slits in the chicken breast

2. Take a small bowl and whisk in olive oil, salt, lemon juice, garlic, paprika, pepper, and whisk for 30 seconds

3. Place chicken in a large bowl and pour marinade

4. Rub the marinade all over using your hand

5. Refrigerate overnight

6. Preheat grill to medium heat and oil the grate

7. Cook chicken in the grill until the center is no longer pink

8. Serve and enjoy!

Nutrition (Per Serving)

- Calories: 644
- Fat: 57g
- Carbohydrates: 2g
- Protein: 27g

Chicken Ham And Turnip Pasta

Serving: 4

Prep Time: 10 minutes

Cook Time: 10 minutes

Ingredients

- 6 slices chicken ham, chopped
- 1 lb turnips, spiralized
- 1 tbsp smoked paprika
- Salt and black pepper to taste
- 4 tbsp olive oil

How To

1. Preheat oven to 450 F. Pour turnips into a bowl; add in the paprika, salt, and pepper; toss to coat.

2. Spread the mixture on a greased baking sheet, scatter ham on top, and drizzle with olive oil.

3. Bake for 10 minutes until golden brown

Nutrition (Per Serving)

- Calories: 191
- Fat: 14g
- Carbohydrates: 10g
- Protein: 9g

The Perfect Winter Turkey Goulash

Serving: 4

Prep Time: 10 minutes

Cook Time: 40-50 minutes

Ingredients

- 2 tablespoons olive oil
- 1 large-sized leek, chopped
- 2 cloves garlic, minced
- 2 pounds turkey thighs, skinless, boneless, and chopped
- 2 celery stalks, chopped

How To

1. Heat the olive oil in a soup pot over a moderate flame. Then, sweat the leeks until just tender and fragrant.
2. Then, cook the garlic until aromatic.
3. Add in the turkey thighs and celery; add 4 cups of water and bring to a boil. Immediately reduce the heat and allow it to simmer for 35 to 40 minutes.
4. Ladle into individual bowls and serve hot.

Nutrition (Per Serving)

- Calories: 220
- Fat: 8g
- Carbohydrates: 2g
- Protein: 35g

Chapter 4 : Beef Recipes

Mushroom And Olive "Mediterranean" Steak

Serving: 4

Prep Time: 10 minutes

Cook Time: 14 minutes

Ingredients

- 1 pound boneless beef sirloin steak, ¾ inch thick, cut into 4 pieces
- 1 large red onion, chopped
- 1 cup mushrooms

- 4 garlic cloves, thinly sliced
- 4 tablespoons olive oil
- ½ cup green olives, coarsely chopped
- 1 cup parsley leaves, finely cut

How To

1. Take a large-sized skillet and place it over medium-high heat

2. Add oil and let it heat p

3. Add beef and cook until both sides are browned, remove beef and drain fat

4. Add rest of the oil to skillet and heat it up

5. Add onions, garlic and cook for 2-3 minutes

6. Stir well

7. Add mushrooms olives and cook until mushrooms are thoroughly done

8. Return beef to skillet and lower heat to medium

9. Cook for 3-4 minutes (covered_

10. Stir in parsley

11. Serve and enjoy!

Nutrition (Per Serving)

- Calories: 386
- Fat: 30g
- Carbohydrates: 11g
- Protein: 21g

Satisfying Low-Carb Beef Liver Salad

Serving: 3

Prep Time: 10 minutes

Cook Time: Nil

Ingredients

- 3-4 ounces beef liver, cooked
- 1 egg, hard-boiled
- 1 ounce dried mushroom
- 1 whole onion, minced
- 2 ounces mayonnaise
- 2 ounces olive oil

- Salt and pepper to taste
- Dill for serving
- ½ a red bell pepper, sliced

How To

1. Cut mushroom and livers into strips and transfer to a bowl

2. Peel the egg and slice it, transfer to a bowl

3. Add remaining ingredients and toss well

4. Sprinkle with dill and serve!

Nutrition (Per Serving)

- Calories: 300
- Fat: 26g
- Carbohydrates: 5g
- Protein: 10g

Perfect Aromatic Beef Roast

Serving: 4

Prep Time: 10 minutes

Cook Time: 50 minutes

Ingredients

- 1 lb of beef sirloin or similar lean cut for roast
- 2 tbsp of mustard
- 2 tbsp of olive oil
- 2 tbsp of garlic salt
- 1 spring of fresh rosemary

How To

1. Combine the mustard, olive oil, and garlic salt in a small bowl.

2. Take the roast beef, remove excess fat and make small incisions lengthwise so you can let the mixture penetrate more easily.

3. Brush the mustard mixture over the beef, making sure it all nicely coated.

4. Place on a baking dish and arrange the rosemary leaves on the sides for extra aroma.

5. Cook in a preheated oven at 380F/180 C for 50 minutes (for a medium cook inside).

6. Serve with mashed sweet potatoes and/or salad

Nutrition (Per Serving)

- Calories: 646
- Fat: 27g
- Carbohydrates: 0.1g
- Protein: 96g

Beef Packed Zucchini Boats

Serving: 4

Prep Time: 10 minutes

Cook Time: 30 minutes

Ingredients

- 1 lb of ground beef with around 80% meat and 20% fat ratio
- 1 cup of red Mexican salsa
- 4 medium zucchinis
- 1/2 shredded cheddar cheese
- 1 tbsp of olive oil

How To

1. Take the zucchinis, cut in half lengthwise, and scoop out the middle flesh inside (leaving enough flesh to make a boat on the sides). Take a form and pinch the insides slightly.

2. Heat the pan with olive oil and add the ground beef.

3. Sauté for 7-8 minutes or until most of the juices have evaporated.

4. Add the salsa and cook for another couple of minutes

5. Distribute the ground beef and salsa over the zucchini boats

6. Sprinkle with the cheese on top of each.

7. Bake in the oven for 15 minutes and serve

Nutrition (Per Serving)

- Calories: 280
- Fat: 13g
- Carbohydrates: 4.2g
- Protein: 30g

Spicy Chipotle Steak

Serving: 4

Prep Time: 10 minutes

Cook Time: 10-20 minutes

Ingredients

- 2 sirloin steaks, cut into thin strips
- 1 tbsp of chipotle seasoning powder
- 2 tbsp of olive oil
- 1/4 cup tomato paste
- Salt to taste

How To

1. Combine the tomato paste, olive oil, and chipotle seasoning with salt to make a marinade.

2. Brush the mixture onto the steaks.

3. Heat a grilling pan and cook the steaks 2-3 minutes on each side for medium inside or depending on how cooked you want them to be

Nutrition (Per Serving)

- Calories: 470
- Fat: 24g
- Carbohydrates: 4g
- Protein: 50g

Chapter 5 : Fish and Seafood Recipes

Grilled Lime Shrimp

Serving: 8

Prep Time: 25 minutes

Cook Time: 5 minutes

Ingredients

- 1 pound medium shrimp, peeled and deveined
- 1 lime, juiced
- ½ cup olive oil
- 3 tablespoons Cajun seasoning

How To

1. Take a re-sealable zip bag and add lime juice, Cajun seasoning, olive oil
2. Add shrimp and shake it well, let it marinate for 20 minutes
3. Preheat your outdoor grill to medium heat
4. Lightly grease the grate
5. Remove shrimp from marinade and cook for 2 minutes per side
6. Serve and enjoy!

Nutrition (Per Serving)

- Calories: 188
- Fat: 3g
- Net Carbohydrates: 1.2g
- Protein: 13g

Mouthwatering Calamari

Serving: 4

Prep Time: 10 minutes +1-hour marinating

Cook Time: 8 minutes

Ingredients

- 2 tablespoons extra virgin olive oil
- 1 teaspoon chili powder
- ½ teaspoon ground cumin
- Zest of 1 lime
- Juice of 1 lime
- Dash of sea salt

- 1 and ½ pounds squid, cleaned and split open, with tentacles cut into ½ inch rounds
- 2 tablespoons cilantro, chopped
- 2 tablespoons red bell pepper, minced

How To

1. Take a medium bowl and stir in olive oil, chili powder, cumin, lime zest, sea salt, lime juice, and pepper

2. Add squid and let it marinade and stir to coat, coat and let it refrigerate for 1 hour

3. Preheat your oven to broil

4. Arrange squid on a baking sheet, broil for 8 minutes turn once until tender

5. Garnish the broiled calamari with cilantro and red bell pepper

6. Serve and enjoy!

Nutrition (Per Serving)

- Calories: 159
- Fat: 13g
- Carbohydrates: 12g
- Protein: 3g

Salmon And Zesty Cream Sauce

Serving: 4

Prep Time: 10 minutes

Cook Time: 5-7 minutes

Ingredients

- 2 boneless salmon or trout fillets
- 1/3 cup sour cream
- 2 tsp mustard
- 1 tbsp lemon juice
- 1/2 tsp dill
- 1 tsp lemon zest

How To

1. Mix all the cream ingredients and spices together in a small bowl.

2. Season with salt and pepper to taste and set aside.

3. Lightly grease a shallow pan and cook the fillets for 2-3 minutes on each side (for a medium to well-done result).

4. Serve on a dish and pour the sauce on top or the side. You can serve it also with some broccoli or asparagus for an extra kick of taste and nutrients

Nutrition (Per Serving)

- Calories: 397
- Fat: 22g
- Carbohydrates: 4g
- Protein: 42g

Crisped Up Coconut Shrimp

Serving: 4

Prep Time: 10 minutes

Cook Time: 20 minutes

Ingredients

- 1 pound of large shrimp (peeled and deveined)
- ½ cup coconut flour
- 1 tsp cayenne seasoning (salt included)
- 3 eggs beaten
- 1/2 cup unsweetened coconut flakes

How To

1. Keep the coconut flour with the seasoning, coconut flakes, and beaten eggs into separate bowls each.

2. Dip and roll in the shrimps (one by one) into the coconut flour mixture, shake off the excess flour, dip in the eggs and then roll in last to the unsweetened coconut flakes.

3. Heat one cup of oil and fry the shrimps for 4-5 minutes or until golden brown.

4. Serve in a shallow dish with absorbing paper and serve with hot mayo (mayo with cayenne seasoning)

Nutrition (Per Serving)

- Calories: 354
- Fat: 24g
- Carbohydrates: 20g
- Protein: 13g

Spiced Up Tuna Avocado Balls

Serving: 4

Prep Time: 10 minutes

Cook Time: Nil

Ingredients

- 2 avocados halved
- $1/2$ lb of sushi-grade ahi tuna (or smoked tuna if you can't find any)
- 2 tbsp of mayo
- 1-2 sriracha sauce
- 1 tsp of toasted sesame seeds

How To

1. Combine in a small bowl the tuna with the mayo, sriracha sauce, and toasted sesame seeds.

2. Scoop and distribute the mixture onto the avocado halves.

3. Add some extra sriracha sauce optionally on top

Nutrition (Per Serving)

- Calories: 256
- Fat: 17g
- Carbohydrates: 8g
- Protein: 15g

Chapter 6 : Soups and Stews Recipes

Clean Chicken And Mushroom Stew

Serving: 4

Prep Time: 10 minutes

Cook Time: 35 minutes

Ingredients

- 4 chicken breast halves, cut into bite-sized pieces
- 1 pound mushrooms, sliced (5-6 cups)
- 1 bunch spring onion, chopped
- 4 tablespoons olive oil
- 1 teaspoon thyme
- Salt and pepper as needed

How To

1. Take a large deep frying pan and place it over medium-high heat
2. Add oil and let it heat up
3. Add chicken and cook for 4-5 minutes per side until slightly browned
4. Add spring onions and mushrooms, season with salt and pepper according to your taste
5. Stir
6. Cover with lid and bring the mix to a boil
7. Lower heat and simmer for 25 minutes
8. Serve!

Nutrition (Per Serving)

- Calories: 247
- Fat: 12g
- Carbohydrates: 10g
- Protein: 23g

Hearty Keto Chicken And Egg Soup

Serving: 2

Prep Time: 5 minutes

Cook Time: 10 minutes

Ingredients

- 1 and ½ cup chicken broth
- 2 whole eggs
- 1 teaspoon chili garlic paste
- 1 tablespoon bacon grease
- ½ a cube, chicken bouillon

How To

1. Take a stovetop pan and place it over medium-high heat
2. Add chicken broth, bouillon cube, bacon grease, and stir
3. Bring the mix to a boil
4. Mix in chili garlic paste
5. Take a bowl and whisk in eggs, add whisked egg to the pan
6. Lower down the heat and gently simmer for a few minutes
7. Serve and enjoy!

Nutrition (Per Serving)

- Calories: 280
- Fat: 25g
- Carbohydrates: 3g
- Protein: 14g

Ingenious Eggplant Soup

Serving: 8

Prep Time: 20 minutes

Cook Time: 15 minutes

Ingredients

- 1 large eggplant, washed and cubed
- 1 tomato, seeded and chopped
- 1 small onion, diced
- 2 tablespoons parsley, chopped
- 2 tablespoons extra virgin olive oil
- 2 tablespoons distilled white vinegar
- ½ cup parmesan cheese, crumbled

- Salt as needed

How To

1. Preheat your outdoor grill to medium-high
2. Pierce the eggplant a few times using a knife/fork
3. Cook the eggplants on your grill for about 15 minutes until they are charred
4. Keep it on the side and allow them to cool
5. Remove the skin from the eggplant and dice the pulp
6. Transfer the pulp to the mixing bowl and add parsley, onion, tomato, olive oil, feta cheese, and vinegar
7. Mix well and chill for 1 hour
8. Season with salt and enjoy!

Nutrition (Per Serving)

- Calories: 99
- Fat: 7g
- Carbohydrates: 7g
- Protein:3.4g

Amazing Roasted Carrot Soup

Serving: 4

Prep Time: 10 minutes

Cook Time: 50 minutes

Ingredients

- 8 large carrot, swashed and peeled
- 6 tablespoons olive oil
- 1-quart broth
- Cayenne pepper to taste
- Salt and pepper to taste

How To

1. Preheat your oven to 425 degrees F
2. Take a baking sheet and add carrots, drizzle olive oil, and roast for 30-45 minutes
3. Put roasted carrots into a blender and add broth, puree
4. Pour into saucepan and heat soup
5. Season with salt, pepper, and cayenne
6. Drizzle olive oil
7. Serve and enjoy!

Nutrition (Per Serving)

- Calories: 222
- Fat: 18g
- Net Carbohydrates: 7g
- Protein: 5g

The Brussels's Fever

Serving: 4

Prep Time: 10 minutes

Cook Time: 20 minutes

Ingredients

- 2 tablespoons olive oil
- 1 yellow onion, chopped
- 2 pounds Brussels sprouts, trimmed and halved
- 4 cups chicken stock
- ¼ cup coconut cream

How To

1. Take a pot and place it over medium heat
2. Add oil and let it heat up
3. Add onion and stir cook for 3 minutes
4. Add Brussels sprouts and stir, cook for 2 minutes
5. Add stock and black pepper, stir and bring to a simmer
6. Cook for 20 minutes more
7. Use an immersion blender to make the soup creamy
8. Add coconut cream and stir well
9. Ladle into soup bowls and serve
10. Enjoy!

Nutrition (Per Serving)

- Calories: 200
- Fat: 11g
- Carbohydrates: 6g
- Protein: 11g

Chapter 7 : Vegan and Vegetarian Recipes

Hearty Green Bean Roast

Serving: 4

Prep Time: 10 minutes

Cook Time: 20 minutes

Ingredients

　　1 whole egg

　　2 tablespoons olive oil

　　Salt and pepper to taste

　　1 pound fresh green beans

5 and ½ tablespoons grated parmesan cheese

How To

1. Preheat your oven to 400 degrees F

2. Take a bowl and whisk in eggs with oil and spices

3. Add beans and mix well

4. Stir in parmesan cheese and pour the mix into baking pan (lined with parchment paper)

5. Bake for 15-20 minutes

6. Serve warm and enjoy!

Nutrition (Per Serving)

- Calories: 216
- Fat: 21g
- Carbohydrates: 7g
- Protein: 9g

Almond And Blistered Beans

Serving: 4

Prep Time: 10 minutes

Cook Time: 20 minutes

Ingredients

- 1 pound fresh green beans, ends trimmed
- 1 and ½ tablespoon olive oil
- ¼ teaspoon salt
- 1 and ½ tablespoons fresh dill, minced
- Juice of 1 lemon
- ¼ cup crushed almonds
- Salt as needed

How To

1. Preheat your oven to 400 degrees F

2. Add in the green beans with your olive oil and also with salt

3. Then spread them in one single layer on a large-sized sheet pan

4. Roast it up for 10 minutes and stir it nicely, then roast for another 8-10 minutes

5. Remove it from the oven and keep stirring in the lemon juice alongside the dill

6. Top it up with crushed almonds and some flaky sea salt and serve

Nutrition (Per Serving)

- Calories: 347
- Fat: 16g
- Carbohydrates: 6g
- Protein: 45g

Chipotle Kale Chips

Serving: 4

Prep Time: 4 minutes

Cook Time: 29 minutes

Ingredients

- 2 large bunch kale, chopped into 4 pieces and stemmed
- 1 tablespoon olive oil
- 1/8 teaspoon salt
- 1 teaspoon chipotle powder
- ¼ cup parmesan cheese, shredded

How To

1. Wash kale thoroughly and dry, cut into 4-inch pieces

2. Preheat your oven to 250 degrees F

3. Take a baking sheet and line it with parchment paper

4. Take a bowl and add kale, coat the kale with olive oil, chipotle, and cheese

5. Transfer the mix to a baking sheet

6. Bake for 19 minutes and check the crispiness

7. If you need more crispiness, bake for 9 minutes more

8. Serve and enjoy!

Nutrition (Per Serving)

- Calories: 37
- Fat: 3g
- Carbohydrates: 2g
- Protein: 1g

Classic Guacamole

Serving: 6

Prep Time: 15 minutes

Cook Time: Nil

Ingredients

- 3 large ripe avocados
- 1 large red onion, peeled and diced
- 4 tablespoon of freshly squeezed lime juice
- Salt as needed
- Freshly ground black pepper as needed
- Cayenne pepper as needed

How To

1. Halve the avocados and discard the stone

2. Scoop flesh from 3 avocado halves and transfer to a large bowl

3. Mash using fork

4. Add 2 tablespoon of lime juice and mix

5. Dice the remaining avocado flesh (remaining half) and transfer to another bowl

6. Add remaining juice and toss

7. Add diced flesh with the mashed flesh and mix

8. Add chopped onions and toss

9. Season with salt, pepper, and cayenne pepper

10. Serve and enjoy!

Nutrition (Per Serving)

- Calories: 172
- Fat: 15g
- Carbohydrates: 11g
- Protein: 2g

Astonishingly Simple Lettuce Salad

Serving: 2

Prep Time: 10 minutes

Cook Time: Nil minutes

Ingredients

- 2 ounces Romaine lettuce
- ½ ounce butter
- 1 ounce Adam cheese, sliced
- ½ avocado, sliced
- 1 cherry tomato, sliced
- 1 red bell pepper, sliced

How To

1. Add butter on top of each lettuce leaves

2. Add alternating layers of cheese, avocado, tomato slices

3. Serve and enjoy!

Nutrition (Per Serving)

- Calories: 104
- Fat: 14g
- Carbohydrates: 4g
- Protein: 4g

Chapter 8 : Desserts Recipes

The Easy "No-Bake" Fudge

Serving: 25

Prep Time: 15 minutes + chill time

Cook Time: 5 minutes

Ingredients

- 1 and ¾ cups coconut butter
- 1 cup pumpkin puree
- 1 teaspoon ground cinnamon
- ¼ teaspoon ground nutmeg
- 1 tablespoon coconut oil

How To

1. Take an 8x8 inch square baking pan and line it up with aluminum foil

2. Take a spoon and scoop out coconut butter into a heated pan and allow the butter to melt

3. Keep stirring well and remove the heat once fully melted

4. Add spices and pumpkin and keep straining until you have a grain-like texture

5. Add coconut oil and keep stirring to incorporate everything

6. Scoop the mixture into your baking pan and evenly distribute it

7. Place a wax paper on top of the mixture and press gently to straighten the top

8. Remove the paper and discard

9. Allow it to chill for 1-2 hours

10. Once chilled, take it out and slice it up into pieces

11. Enjoy!

Nutrition (Per Serving)

- Calories: 120
- Fat: 10g
- Carbohydrates: 5g
- Protein: 1.2g

Elegant Poppyseed Muffins

Serving: 6

Prep Time: 10 minutes

Cook Time: 10-15 minutes

Ingredients

- ¾ cup blanched almond flour
- ¼ cup golden flaxseed meal
- 1/3 cup Erythritol
- 1 teaspoon baking powder
- 2 tablespoons poppy seeds
- ¼ cup melted salted butter
- ¼ cup heavy cream
- 3 large whole eggs
- Zest of 2 lemons

- 3 tablespoons lemon juice
- 1 teaspoon vanilla extract
- 25 drops liquid stevia

How To

1. Preheat your oven to a temperature of 350 degrees Fahrenheit

2. Take a mixing bowl and add poppy seeds, almond flour, Erythritol

3. Add the Flaxseed meal as well and let it stir completely

4. Add the melted butter

5. Pour heavy cream alongside egg

6. Mix everything well

7. Add baking powder, vanilla, lemon juice, stevia, and zest

8. Mix everything to incorporate them well

9. Pour the batter into cupcake molds and bake for 20 minutes until a brown texture is seen

10. Cool the muffins on a cooling rack for 10 minutes and serve!

Nutrition (Per Serving)

- Calories: 295
- Fat: 32g
- Carbohydrates: 4g
- Protein: 1g

Swirly Cinnamon Muffins

Serving: 6

Prep Time: 10 minutes

Cook Time: 10-15 minutes

Ingredients

- 1 cup cauliflower, cooked and cooled
- ¾ cup Keto-Friendly Protein Powder
- ½ cup ground peanuts
- 3 egg
- 1 tablespoon coconut oil
- 4 teaspoons stevia
- 1 teaspoon baking powder

- 2 tablespoons Ghee, melted
- 1 tablespoon cinnamon

How To

1. Preheat your oven to 350 degrees F
2. Grease muffin tin
3. Add cauliflower, peanut butter, powder, eggs, coconut oil, baking powder, stevia to a bowl and mix, keep it on the side
4. Pour batter into muffin tins
5. Take a bowl and add cinnamon and ghee, pour ½ teaspoon of the mix on top of each muffin and swirl using a toothpick
6. Bake for 10 minutes
7. Remove from oven and let them cool
8. Serve and enjoy!

Nutrition (Per Serving)

- Calories: 424
- Fat: 27g
- Carbohydrates: 10g
- Protein: 36g

Mesmerizing Garlic Bagels

Serving: 6

Prep Time: 10 minutes

Cook Time: 15 minutes

Ingredients

- 6 whole eggs
- 1 and ½ teaspoon Garlic powder
- 1/3 cup butter, melted
- ½ teaspoon salt
- ½ cup coconut flour sifted
- ½ teaspoon baking powder

How To

1. Preheat your oven to 400 degrees F

2. Grease the bagel pan and keep it on the side

3. Whisk in eggs, garlic powder, butter, salt to a bowl and keep it on the side

4. Add coconut flour and baking powder to the egg mix, mix well until incorporated and a batter forms with no lumps

5. Pour batter into bagel pan

6. Bake for 15 minutes

7. Remove from oven and let them cool

8. Serve and enjoy!

Nutrition (Per Serving)

- Calories: 193
- Fat: 15g
- Carbohydrates: 7g
- Protein: 8g

Ravaging Blueberry Muffin

Serving: 4

Prep Time: 10 minutes

Cook Time: 30 minutes

Ingredients

- 1 cup almond flour
- Pinch of salt
- 1/8 teaspoon baking soda
- 1 whole egg
- 2 tablespoons coconut oil, melted
- ½ cup coconut milk
- ¼ cup fresh blueberries

How To

1. Preheat your oven to 350 degrees F

2. Line a muffin tin with paper muffin cups

3. Add almond flour, salt, baking soda to a bowl and mix, keep it on the side

4. Take another bowl and add egg, coconut oil, coconut milk, and mix

5. Add mix to flour mix and gently combine until incorporated

6. Mix in blueberries and fill the cupcakes tins with batter

7. Bake for 20-25 minutes

8. Enjoy!

Nutrition (Per Serving)

- Calories: 167
- Fat: 15g
- Carbohydrates: 2.1g
- Protein: 5.2g

No-Bake Cheesecake

Serving: 10

Prep Time: 120 minutes

Cook Time: Nil

Ingredients

For Crust

- 2 tablespoons ground flaxseeds
- 2 tablespoons desiccated coconut
- 1 teaspoon cinnamon

For Filling

- 4 ounces vegan cream cheese
- 1 cup cashews, soaked
- ½ cup frozen blueberries
- 2 tablespoons coconut oil
- 1 tablespoon lemon juice
- 1 teaspoon vanilla extract
- Liquid stevia

How To

1. Take a container and mix in the crust ingredients, mix well

2. Flatten the mixture at the bottom to prepare the crust of your cheesecake

3. Take a blender/ food processor and add the filling ingredients, blend until smooth

4. Gently pour the batter on top of your crust and chill for 2 hours

5. Serve and enjoy!

Nutrition (Per Serving)

- Calories: 182
- Fat: 16g
- Carbohydrates: 4g
- Protein: 3g

Stylish Chocolate Parfait

Serving: 4

Prep Time: 2 hours

Cook Time: nil

Ingredients

- 2 tablespoons cocoa powder
- 1 cup almond milk
- 1 tablespoon chia seeds
- Pinch of salt
- ½ teaspoon vanilla extract

How To

1. Take a bowl and add cocoa powder, almond milk, chia seeds, vanilla extract, and stir

2. Transfer to dessert glass and place in your fridge for 2 hours

3. Top with some berries, serve and enjoy!

Nutrition (Per Serving)

- Calories: 130
- Fat: 5g
- Carbohydrates: 7g
- Protein: 16g

Supreme Matcha Bomb

Serving: 10

Prep Time: 100 minutes

Cook Time: Nil

Ingredients

- 3/4 cup hemp seeds
- ½ cup coconut oil
- 2 tablespoons coconut butter
- 1 teaspoon Matcha powder
- 2 tablespoons vanilla bean extract
- ½ teaspoon mint extract
- Liquid stevia

How To

1. Take your blender/food processor and add hemp seeds, coconut oil, Matcha, vanilla extract, and stevia

2. Blend until you have a nice batter and divide into silicon molds

3. Melt coconut butter and drizzle on top

4. Let the cups chill and enjoy!

Nutrition (Per Serving)

- Calories: 200
- Fat: 20g
- Carbohydrates: 3g
- Protein: 5g

Hearty Almond Bread

Serving: 8

Prep Time: 15 minutes

Cook Time: 60 minutes

Ingredients

- 3 cups almond flour
- 1 teaspoon baking soda
- 2 teaspoons baking powder
- ¼ teaspoon salt
- ¼ cup almond milk
- ½ cup + 2 tablespoons olive oil
- 3 whole eggs

How To

1. Preheat your oven to 300 degrees F
2. Take a 9x5 inch loaf pan and grease, keep it on the side
3. Add listed ingredients to a bowl and pour the batter into the loaf pan
4. Bake for 60 minutes
5. Once baked, remove from oven and let it cool
6. Slice and serve!

Nutrition (Per Serving)

- Calories: 277
- Fat: 21g
- Carbohydrates: 7g
- Protein: 10g

Chapter 9 : Refreshing Drinks And Smoothies

The Summer Hearty Shake

Serving: 2

Prep Time: 5 minutes

Ingredients

- 1 cup frozen blackberries
- ¾ cup Whole milk vanilla yogurt
- ½ cup unsweetened vanilla almond milk
- ½ cup of frozen strawberries
- ½ cup frozen peaches
- 1 tablespoon hemp seeds

- Dash of ground cinnamon

Directions

1. Add all the ingredients except vegetables/fruits first

2. Blend until smooth

3. Add the vegetable/fruits

4. Blend until smooth

5. Add a few ice cubes and serve the smoothie

6. Enjoy!

Nutrition Values

- Calories: 187
- Fat: 6g
- Carbohydrates: 17g
- Protein: 6g

Sweet Protein And Cherry Shake

Serving: 2

Prep Time: 5 minutes

Ingredients

- 1 cup of water
- 3 cups spinach
- 2 bananas, sliced
- 2 cups frozen cherries
- 2 tablespoons cacao powder
- 4 tablespoons hemp seeds, shelled

Directions

1. Add all the ingredients except vegetables/fruits first
2. Blend until smooth
3. Add the vegetable/fruits
4. Blend until smooth
5. Add a few ice cubes and serve the smoothie
6. Enjoy!

Nutrition Values

- Calories: 111
- Fat: 3g
- Carbohydrates: 9g
- Protein: 13g

Iron And Protein Shake

Serving: 2

Prep Time: 5 minutes

Ingredients

- 2 tablespoons favorite sweetened
- 1 cup of water
- ¼ cup hemp seeds
- 2 large bananas, frozen
- 4 cups strawberries, sliced

Directions

1. Add all the ingredients except vegetables/fruits first
2. Blend until smooth
3. Add the vegetable/fruits
4. Blend until smooth
5. Add a few ice cubes and serve the smoothie
6. Enjoy!

Nutrition Values

- Calories: 156
- Fat: 14g
- Carbohydrates: 1g
- Protein: 7g

Flax And Almond Butter Smoothie

Serving: 2

Prep Time: 5 minutes

<u>Ingredients</u>

- 1 teaspoon flax seed
- ½ cup crushed ice
- 3 strawberries
- 1 banana, frozen
- 2 cups spinach
- 2 tablespoons almond butter
- ½ cup plain yogurt

Directions

1. Add all the ingredients except vegetables/fruits first
2. Blend until smooth
3. Add the vegetable/fruits
4. Blend until smooth
5. Add a few ice cubes and serve the smoothie
6. Enjoy!

Nutrition Values

- Calories: 147
- Fat: 7g
- Carbohydrates: 15g
- Protein: 4g

Leeks And Broccoli Cucumber Glass

Serving: 2

Prep Time: 5 minutes

Ingredients

- 1 cup crushed ice
- 1 tablespoon Matcha
- ½ cup leaf lettuce, chopped
- ½ cup lettuce, chopped
- 1 lime, juiced
- 2 cucumbers, diced
- 2 leeks, chopped

- 2 tablespoons cashew butter
- 1 cup broccoli, diced

Directions

1. Add all the ingredients except vegetables/fruits first

2. Blend until smooth

3. Add the vegetable/fruits

4. Blend until smooth

5. Add a few ice cubes and serve the smoothie

6. Enjoy!

Nutrition Values

- Calories: 219
- Fat: 6g
- Carbohydrates: 6g
- Protein: 4g

Zucchini Apple Smoothie

Serving: 2

Prep Time: 5 minutes

Ingredients

- 1 and ½ cups crushed ice
- 1 tablespoon Spirulina
- 1 lemon, juiced
- 1 stalk celery
- ¾ avocado
- 2 apples, quartered
- ½ cup zucchini, diced

Directions

1. Add all the ingredients except vegetables/fruits first
2. Blend until smooth
3. Add the vegetable/fruits
4. Blend until smooth
5. Add a few ice cubes and serve the smoothie
6. Enjoy!

Nutrition Values

- Calories: 80
- Fat: 4g
- Carbohydrates: 11g
- Protein: 2g

Flax And Kiwi Spinach Smoothie

Serving: 2

Prep Time: 5 minutes

Ingredients

- 1 cup crushed ice
- 3 tablespoons ground flax
- 3 kiwis, diced
- 1 stalk celery, chopped
- 1 banana, chopped

- 2 apples, quartered
- 1 cup spinach, chopped

Directions

1. Add all the ingredients except vegetables/fruits first
2. Blend until smooth
3. Add the vegetable/fruits
4. Blend until smooth
5. Add a few ice cubes and serve the smoothie
6. Enjoy!

Nutrition Values

- Calories: 142
- Fat: 7g
- Carbohydrates: 16g
- Protein: 6g

CPSIA information can be obtained
at www.ICGtesting.com
Printed in the USA
BVHW092036230521
607791BV00004BA/727

9 781802 850345